TIP 2 Encourage fluent and flexible reading:

- support your child to read in fluent, expressive phrases, making full use of punctuation and thinking about the meaning.
- help your child learn to read with expression by choosing a sentence to read aloud and demonstrating how to do this.

TIP 3 Indicators that your child is reading for meaning:

- your child will be responding to the text if he/she is self-correcting and varying his/her voice.
- your child will want to talk about what he/she is reading or is eager to turn the page to find out what will happen next.

TIP 4 Chat at the end of each chapter:

- encourage your child to recall specific details after each chapter.
- let your child pick out interesting words and discuss what they mean.
- talk about what each of you found most interesting or most important.
- ask questions about the text. These help to develop comprehension skills and awareness of the language used.

A FEW ADDITIONAL TIPS

- Read to your child regularly to demonstrate fluency, phrasing, and expression; to find out or check information; and for sharing enjoyment.
- Encourage your child to reread favorite texts to increase reading confidence and fluency.
- Check that your child is reading a range of different types of material, such as poems, jokes, and following instructions.

Editor Ellie Barton
Designer Lisa Lanzarini
Art Director Lisa Lanzarini
Publisher Julie Ferris
Publishing Director Simon Beecroft
Pre-Production Producer Kavita Varma
Senior Producer Alex Bell

For Lucasfilm
Executive Editor Jonathan W. Rinzler
Art Director Troy Alders
Keeper of the Holocron Leland Chee
Director of Publishing Carol Roeder

Reading Consultant
Linda B. Gambrell, Ph.D.

First American Edition, 2010
16 17 18 19 10 9 8 7 6 5 4 3 2 1

Published in the United States by DK Publishing
345 Hudson Street, New York, New York 10014

Copyright © 2016 Dorling Kindersley Limited
DK , a Division of Penguin Random House LLC

Published in Great Britain by Dorling Kindersley Limited.

DK books are available at special discounts when purchased in bulk for sales promotions, premiums, fund-raising, or educational use. For details, contact:
DK Publishing Special Markets
345 Hudson Street
New York, New York 10014
SpecialSales@dk.com

A catalog record for this book is available from the Library of Congress.

ISBN: 9781465460042 (Paperback)
ISBN: 9781465460059 (Hardcover)

Printed in China

A WORLD OF IDEAS:
SEE ALL THERE IS TO KNOW
www.dk.com
www.starwars.com

Contents

STAR WARS®

DEATH STAR BATTLES

Written by Simon Beecroft

That's no moon!

You are flying through
deep space.
Suddenly, a small
enemy fighter ship
shoots past.
Where did it
come from?
All you can see
is a small moon
up ahead.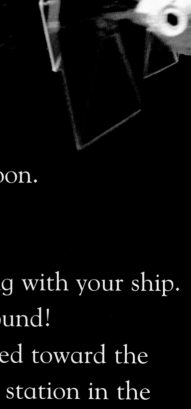
Wait, that's no moon.
It is too big.
Quick, turn back!
Something is wrong with your ship.
It will not turn around!
You are being pulled toward the
most deadly battle station in the
galaxy: the Death Star.

The Death Star is the evil Empire's ultimate weapon. It has a superlaser that is powerful enough to destroy an entire planet with one gigantic blast.

The Death Star
The Death Star has a population of about 1.7 million people and over 400,000 droids.

How to build a Death Star

Only one man in the galaxy is evil
enough to need a planet-destroying
superweapon: Emperor Palpatine.
The Emperor is a vile Sith Lord.
He rules the galaxy alongside Darth
Vader and huge armies of deadly
stormtroopers. The Emperor will do
anything he can to increase
his power.
He plans to use the
Death Star to destroy
his enemies and the
Rebel Alliance.

Tarkin oversees construction of the Death Star with the Emperor and Darth Vader

Grand Moff Tarkin is one of the
Emperor's top commanders.
He masterminded the construction
of the Death Star for Emperor
Palpatine. He used a clever
species of engineers, the
Geonosians, and he forced
many Wookiee slaves and
other prisoners to build the
fearsome weapon.

Conference room

Grand Moff Tarkin and Darth Vader command the Death Star from the overbridge, where they make their sinister plans in a dark room.
The Death Star has a special trained fighting force; Death Star Troopers.

Two Death Star Troopers stand guard during top-level meetings. The Imperial leaders sit around a black table with a holoprojector in the middle, which displays tactical holograms and maps. During meetings Darth Vader sometimes intimidates his officers by using the dark side of the Force.

Fire when ready...

Grand Moff Tarkin and Darth Vader have captured Princess Leia, an important Rebel leader. They want her to tell them the location of the Rebels' hidden base. They threaten to destroy her home planet Alderaan if she refuses. Leia says the base is on a planet called Dantooine. But Tarkin destroys Alderaan anyway to show the Rebels just how powerful the Death Star is.

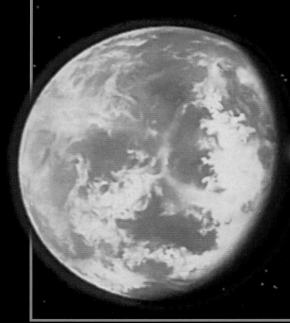

The disk-shaped superweapon blasts out eight beams of light that join together into one powerful laser beam. The small green planet is blown into space dust.

Superlaser

The Death Star's superlaser uses so much energy to fire that it takes 24 hours to recharge before it can be fired again.

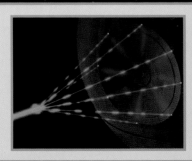

Trapped!

While Leia is held prisoner on the Death Star, Luke Skywalker is on his way to Alderaan. He is traveling in a starship called the *Millennium Falcon*. With him are Jedi Knight Obi-Wan Kenobi, captain Han Solo, a Wookiee named Chewbacca and two droids, C-3PO and R2-D2.

When they arrive where Alderaan used to be, they see a TIE fighter. It heads straight toward a small moon which turns out to be the Death Star.

The Death Star uses an invisible tractor beam to grab hold of Luke's ship so it cannot escape. They are pulled into a docking bay within a mile-high trench that runs around the middle of the Death Star.

Deadly surface

The surface of the Death Star is covered with weapons, including 10,000 turbolaser guns and 2,500 laser cannons. Eight thousand tractor beam projectors can trap enemy ships that come too close.

Into the Death Star

The *Falcon* is forced to land in a giant hangar. An invisible shield across the entrance maintains the artificial atmosphere.

Docking bays

The Death Star has many docking bays for spaceships. Some are designed for visiting ships, others are hangars for Imperial fighters such as TIE.

Beside the ship is a large hole in the floor, which has an elevator to raise and lower ships for repairs.

Control room windows overlook the hangar. They are surrounded by stormtroopers.

Stormtroopers

Stormtroopers are the Empire's elite soldiers. They wear white helmets that cover their faces and suits of armor made up of 18 pieces.
Stormtroopers are armed with blaster pistols or blaster rifles.

A squad of stormtroopers boards the *Falcon*. They are looking for the crew. Luke and the others are hiding in secret compartments beneath the floor.

Tour of duty
At least 25,000 stormtroopers serve on the Death Star at any one time. They patrol every part of the enormous battle station.

I can't see in this helmet!

Han and Luke ambush two
stormtroopers and steal their armor.
Disguised as stormtroopers, they
discover that Princess Leia is a prisoner.

Turbolifts

Elevators, called turbolifts, connect all sectors of the Death Star. Turbolifts move up and down as well as side to side. Some turbolifts are reserved only for officers.

Luke has a plan to rescue her.
They handcuff Chewbacca and pretend he is their prisoner.
Han and Luke try to look relaxed in their stormtrooper disguises as they wait for a turbolift to arrive.
Troops, bureaucrats, and robots move about, but most of them ignore the trio.
Only a few glance at the giant Wookiee.

Prison break

Finally, Luke and Han find the prison block in which Leia is being held. But an Imperial officer becomes suspicious and they have a blaster battle. Once Han and Luke find Leia, more stormtroopers arrive, cutting off their only exit. Han and Luke exchange fire with the stormtroopers.

Interrogator droid
Imperial cell blocks
are horrible places.
Security cameras
spy on prisoners while
interrogator droids
electroshock them
to force them to
answer questions.

Leia has to think very fast now. The
only way out is a garbage chute!

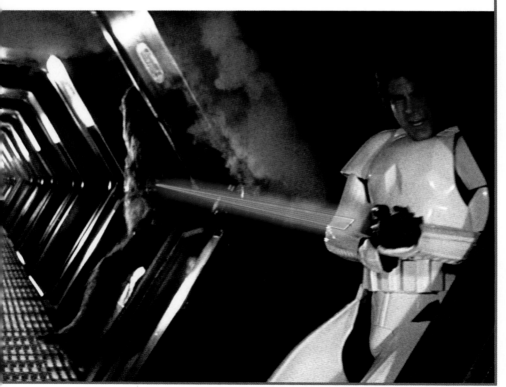

Something is alive in here!

Luke, Leia, Han, and Chewbacca whiz
down the garbage chute and land in
a smelly, dirty trash compactor.
This is where garbage of every kind is
collected before being crushed and
dumped into space. It is totally sealed.

Dianoga serpent
Dianogas, or garbage
squids, live in trash
compactors, refuse pits
and sewers across the
galaxy, feeding on
scraps and rubbish.

When Han tries to blast his way out,
the laserbolt bounces around the small
metal room and nearly hits one of them.
Then they hear a frightening growl and
realize something is living in there.
Suddenly, a long tentacle grabs hold of
Luke and pulls him under!
The others think Luke is gone forever,
but the creature spits him out.
Then the walls start closing in.
They are going to be crushed!

Droids to the rescue

Luke shouts into his comlink to get help
from C-3PO and R2-D2.
But in the control room stormtroopers
have discovered the droids.

C-3PO pretends he knows where Luke and the others are and sends the stormtroopers in the opposite direction. R2-D2 is then able to plug into the computer and turn off the trash compactor.

C-3PO can hear his friends screaming and thinks that his friends are being crushed to death. Actually, they are whooping for joy because the walls have stopped closing in. Well done, R2-D2!

Desperate leap

As Luke and Leia are
trying to escape the deadly
stormtroopers, they run
through a doorway—and
nearly fall from a ledge to
their death. Below them is a
deep shaft that appears to go
on forever!

Luke fires at the stormtroopers
while Leia hits a switch that
shuts the door, leaving them
perched on the short ledge.
But the stormtroopers are
opening the door.

On the other side of the chasm, more
stormtroopers begin to blast at them.
Luke fires at the new enemies but then
he has an idea.

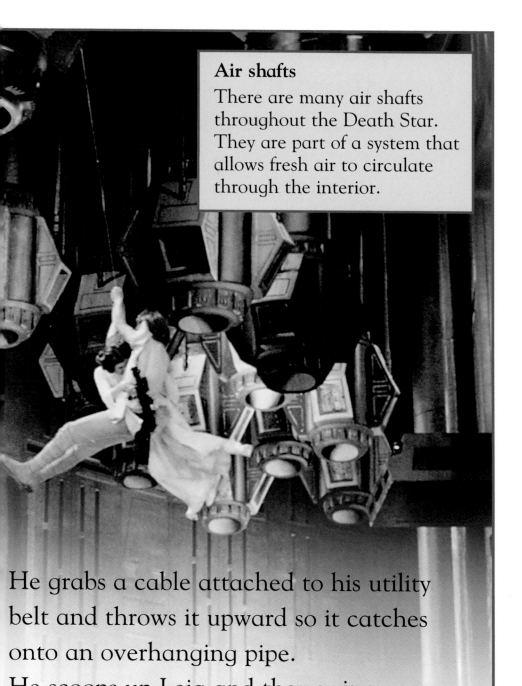

Air shafts

There are many air shafts throughout the Death Star. They are part of a system that allows fresh air to circulate through the interior.

He grabs a cable attached to his utility belt and throws it upward so it catches onto an overhanging pipe.
He scoops up Leia and they swing across to safety!

Solo mission

Machines called reactor couplings power
the huge tractor beam that is preventing
Han's ship from leaving the Death Star.
Obi-Wan knows that if he switches off
one of these machines, he will free
the *Falcon*.

He slips past some stormtroopers using the Force to stay hidden.
Obi-Wan finally reaches the reactor coupling. It stands on a shaft inside a trench that seems to be a hundred miles deep.
The Jedi edges his way along a narrow ledge that leads to a control panel.
He quickly turns off the machines.

Final duel

The most fearsome presence on the Death Star is Darth Vader. His black caped figure walking down the corridor is a terrifying sight. Vader can sense that Obi-Wan Kenobi is on the Death Star and tracks him down. They confront each other. Swoosh! Their lightsabers clash and spark!

Lost friendship
Darth Vader is a Sith Lord who was once a Jedi
Knight called Anakin. Anakin is Luke's father.
Obi-Wan was Anakin's Master until Anakin
became a Sith. Anakin fought Obi-Wan, but
lost. He has wanted revenge since then.

Luke watches Obi-Wan block Vader's
every move, until the old Jedi Master
stands still with a calm look on his face.
Vader strikes down Kenobi with a single
slash of his blade. Obi-Wan's cloak falls
to the floor, but he is not in it.
Luke cries out, "No!" as Vader prods the
empty robe with his foot.

We are not safe yet!

Thanks to Obi-Wan, the *Falcon* blasts off from the deadly Death Star. But TIE fighters give chase. Luke and Han work together, manning their turbolasers and blowing up all the enemy ships.

Han and Luke are relieved, but Leia thinks Tarkin has let them escape. Leia is right—Tarkin is tracking their ship. He still wants to find out the location of the Rebels' hidden base.

X-wings

X-wings are starfighters. They have four wings, called S-foils, which form the shape of an 'X'. They are made by a company called Incom.

Rebel attack

The Death Star is more powerful than half the entire firepower of the Imperial Starfleet. But the Rebels think they have found a way to destroy it.

Rebel briefing
At the Rebel base on Yavin 4, the Rebels study the Death Star plans that R2-D2 has been carrying. Leia knows that the Rebels must act fast if they want to outsmart Vader.

The rebels fly along a narrow tunnel on the surface of the Death Star.

At the end of the tunnel is an exhaust port. If they can fire a laser bolt right into this tiny hole, the bolt will penetrate the main reactor.

This would start a chain reaction that would destroy the station.

The Rebels hope that their ships are small enough to avoid the Death Star's outer defenses, which are designed to stop large-scale assaults.

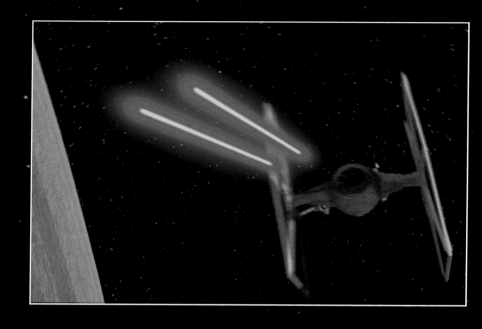

Turbolaser defense

The Death Star has powerful turbolasers, but the starfighters are nimble. The Death Star's defenses are also not strong enough against the Force.

When Obi-Wan tells Luke to "use the Force" instead of his targeting computer, Luke fires two proton torpedos into the Reactor Core.

he battle station is destroyed before
can attack the Rebel base.
It the sinister Emperor will not let this
op him. He has a plan...

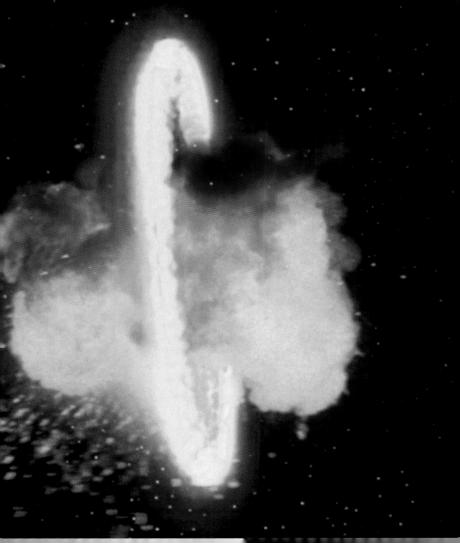

The second Death Star

After the destruction of the Death Star at the Battle of Yavin, Emperor Palpatine orders the construction of a second Death Star. This battle station is even larger than the first, with thousands more turbolasers. The second Death Star also has a planet-destroying superlaser, which can be recharged in just three minutes! This superlaser can also fire at small targets, such as enemy ships. It is more powerful and accurate.
The Emperor is sure that, this time, he will crush forever the Rebel rebellion.

Emperor Palpatine arrives

The Emperor's personal shuttle lands on the new Death Star. He has arrived to inspect the new battle station.

He is greeted by Darth Vader.
Hundreds of stormtroopers line
up and the Imperial Red Guards
bow to him.

The Emperor wants this Death
Star to look unfinished in order to
trick the Rebels into attacking.
When the Rebels attack, the
Emperor intends to destroy their
fleet once and for all!

Final battle

Just as the Emperor planned, the Rebels decide to attack the second Death Star because it seems weak and unprotected. Lando Calrissian leads the Rebel fleet.

He is Han's friend and flies the *Falcon*. The Rebels don't know it is a trap. Meanwhile, Palpatine tricks Luke into battle with Darth Vader. Luke defeats his father—but refuses to kill him. So, the Emperor unleashes unstoppable Sith lightning at Luke. At the last moment, Darth hurls the Emperor into an abyss, saving Luke's life.

Most powerful Jedi
Because Luke feels compassion for his father, Darth Vader, he reveals himself to be the most powerful Jedi of them all.

Battle of Endor

A Rebel team, led by Han Solo and
Princess Leia, destroys the shield
generator protecting the Death Star.
This allows the *Falcon* to fly into its
interior, chased by TIE fighters.

Lando and his friends blast away at the main reactor.
The Death Star explodes!
Emperor Palpatine is dead.
All over the galaxy, people celebrate their new freedom.

Big explosion
The second Death Star becomes a ball of flames and the *Falcon* flies away. The Rebels have won!

A New Threat

The galaxy is not safe for long.
Many years after the second Death
Star is destroyed, the Empire is back.
Now they call themselves the First
Order – and they want revenge!

The First Order has built a
superweapon called the Starkiller.
It is much bigger than the Death
Star. It can destroy entire star
systems with a single, powerful blast.

Princess Leia leads a group
of rebels against the First Order.

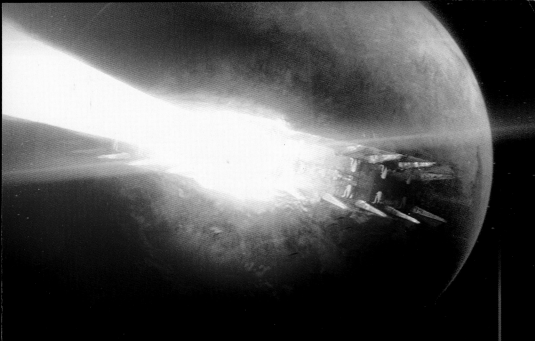

Once again, the rebel pilots must jump into their starfighters.
The battle against the dark side is never over…

Dark Warrior
The First Order's greatest warrior is Kylo Ren. He is Princess Leia's son and he has turned to the dark side. Kylo Ren wants to be even deadlier than his grandfather, Darth Vader!

Glossary

Ambush
A surprise attack made by people from a hiding place.

Armor
Protective clothing.

Artificial
Fake or not real.

Bureaucrat
An office worker.

Chain Reaction
An event that leads to another important event happening.

Engineer
A person who designs and makes machinery or vehicles.

Enormous
Unusually big.

Fearsome
Very frightening.

The Force
A mysterious energy that can be used for good or evil.

Geonosian
Insectoid race from the planet Geonosis.

Hangar
A large, warehouse building or room for housing spaceships or vehicles.

Holoprojector
A device that projects a hologram.

Nimble
Fast and able to change direction quickly.

Reactor Coupling
The system that powers the tractor beams.

Sinister
Very bad, mysterious, and scary.

Sith Lord
A leader of the evil Siths who use the dark side of the Force.

Slave
Someone who is owned by a master and is forced to do everything they are told to.

Stormtrooper
Members of the Emperor's personal army.

Tentacle
The long, flexible legs and arms of a creature with many limbs.

Terrifying
Extremely scary and frightening.

Tractor Beam
A beam that can pull one object toward another.